SUPERWOMEN in STEM

Women scientists in Physics and Engineering

CATHERINE BRERETON

raintree

a Capstone company — publishers for children

Raintree is an imprint of Capstone Global Library Limited, a company incorporated in England and Wales having its registered office at 264 Banbury Road, Oxford, OX2 7DY – Registered company number: 6695582

www.raintree.co.uk
myorders@raintree.co.uk

© Brown Bear Books Ltd 2021
This edition published by Raintree in 2021

Created by Brown Bear Books Ltd
Text and Editor: Nancy Dickmann
Designer and Illustrator: Supriya Sahai
Editorial Director: Lindsey Lowe
Children's Publisher: Anne O'Daly
Design Manager: Keith Davis
Picture Manager: Sophie Mortimer
Printed and bound in India

ISBN 978 1 4747 9863 1 (hardback)
ISBN 978 1 4747 9869 3 (paperback)

British Library Cataloguing in Publication Data
A full catalogue record for this book is available from the British Library

Concept development: Square and Circus / Brown Bear Books Ltd

Picture Credits
Alamy: Science History Images 20; Getty Images: CBS Photo Archive 35t, Keystone Features/Stringer 28, George Rinhart 26; istockphoto: Nicolas McComber 38; Library of Congress: 9, 41t; National Museum of American History: 40; Public Domain: 10, 11, 23, 27, 32, 34, Arte Publicidad 8, Energy.gov 21, The New Yorker 41b, Nuclear Fission Deutsches Museum/J Brew 17, Smithsonian Institution Archives 14, 17b; Robert Hunt Library: 33; Science and Society Picture Library: Daily Herald Archive 39; Shutterstock: 35b, Ezume Images 17t, Peter Hermes Furian 15, indukas 5, Murat Hajdarhodzic 4, Anna Om 29; Thinkstock: Robin Mac 22.

Character artwork © Supriya Sahai
All other artwork © Brown Bear Books Ltd

Every effort has been made to contact copyright holders of material reproduced in this book. Any omissions will be rectified in subsequent printings if notice is given to the publisher.

All the internet addresses (URLs) given in this book were valid at the time of going to press. However, due to the dynamic nature of the internet, some addresses may have changed, or sites may have changed or ceased to exist since publication. While the author and publisher regret any inconvenience this may cause readers, no responsibility for any such changes can be accepted by either the author or the publisher.

contents

The study of matter

Physics is a curiosity about the world and a desire to understand what makes it tick. It is also a drive to invent: to create tools, machines and feats of engineering.

From ancient times, people have studied the universe and everything in it. This is physics – the study of matter (the stuff everything is made of) and energy, and the relationships between them. Also from the earliest times, people have put their minds to work as engineers, devising inventions to allow them to carry out tasks from ploughing fields to bridging rivers and firing weapons.

The first engineer we know of by name is Imhotep. engineer of this pyramid at Saqarra. Egypt.

Physicists today continue the search to uncover the secrets of the universe.

MAKING SENSE OF MATTER

The ancient Greek thinker Aristotle was the first to use the term "physics", writing about motion, gravity and the planets. In the 1500s, Galileo Galilei made new discoveries about how the planets move. He is sometimes called the "father of physics", although the title is also given to Isaac Newton, who came up with a theory of gravity, or Albert Einstein, whose theory of relativity is one of the greatest scientific achievements.

EXAMINING ATOMS

From the late 1700s, scientists made advances in the study of atoms – the tiny particles that are the basic units of matter – and women played a vital role. Lise Meitner and Maria Goeppert Mayer made discoveries crucial to the understanding of atoms. Much of physics today is about unlocking the secrets of how atoms behave. And just as exciting as scientific theory are the practical applications of physics, from electrical engineering, to construction, communications and inventions for the home. Despite facing huge obstacles, women have had a crucial part in the development of the study of physics and engineering.

Hertha Ayrton

British physicist Hertha Ayrton invented a new kind of electric streetlight and blazed a trail for women electrical engineers and inventors.

Hertha Ayrton was born Phoebe Sarah Marks on 28 April 1854, near Portsmouth in the United Kingdom. She was one of eight children – her father was a Polish Jewish immigrant watchmaker and her mother was a seamstress. The family struggled to make a living, but Hertha was lucky enough to get an education. At the age of nine she moved to London to become a pupil at her aunt's school. She had lessons in French and music, and learned maths and Latin from her cousins. She started working as a governess at the age of 16.

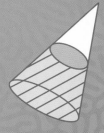

QUICK FACTS

....

NAME: born Phoebe
Sarah Marks – Hertha
was a nickname she
adopted and Ayrton
was her married name

BIRTH: 1854, near
Portsmouth, UK

OCCUPATION: Engineer,
physicist, mathematician,
inventor

EDUCATION: Cambridge
University, University
of London

> **66** Errors are notoriously hard to kill, but an error that ascribes to a man what was actually the work of a woman has more lives than a cat. **99**

MATHS MENTOR

While working as a governess, Hertha met Barbara Bodichon, a wealthy woman who supported female education. Madame Bodichon was impressed with Hertha's ability at maths, so she paid for her to have advanced maths lessons, and later for her to go to Girton College, Cambridge. This was the first women's university college in the UK, co-founded by Madame Bodichon herself.

SPARKS OF SCIENCE

Hertha was studying maths, but soon found the sparks of the interest that would drive her: science and invention. She devised a line divider that could be used to mark out a line into any number of equal parts. This was useful for engineers and architects. The invention received a lot of press attention.

Hertha had to struggle to get her work recognized. She was friends with Marie Curie, also a star female physicist with Polish roots.

Hertha supported Madame Bodichon's work for the suffragette movement, which campaigned for women to get the vote.

In 1884, Hertha began attending a technical college in London, to learn about electricity. The teacher was Professor William Ayrton, a pioneer of electrical engineering and a Fellow of the Royal Society. William became Hertha's husband and inventing partner.

A QUIET, BRIGHT LIGHT

In the 1890s, electric streetlights made a hissing sound. Hertha and William wanted to improve the technology, but it was Hertha who made the breakthrough. One day she was going through William's research papers and trying to repeat some of his experiments when she made an important discovery. She realized that the hissing noise was from a type of chemical reaction called oxidation. This discovery meant that she was able to invent a new arc that made a quiet, bright light.

Hertha is the name of a German earth goddess. Hertha's friends gave her this nickname when she was a young girl, because she was so energetic – a force of nature. She liked the name so much she kept it!

In 2015, Hertha had a prize named for her. The Ayrton prize is for outstanding web projects in the history of science, technology and medicine.

ELECTRICAL SPEAKER

Hertha's invention caused a stir. She gave demonstrations of her new, quiet electric arc. People were amazed by the sight of a woman handling such dangerous-looking electrical equipment. She was the first woman to give a lecture to the Institution of Electrical Engineers (in 1899), the first woman to become a member of the institution and the first to win one of their prizes. She led the physical science section of the International Congress of Women in London in 1899 and spoke at the International Electrical Congress in Paris in 1900.

All this success meant that even the Royal Society – which did not admit women members – eventually allowed Hertha to present a paper. In 1906, they awarded her their top prize, the Hughes Medal, for her work on electricity.

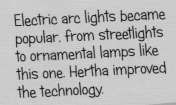

Electric arc lights became popular, from streetlights to ornamental lamps like this one. Hertha improved the technology.

THE AYRTON FAN

From 1883 until just before her death in 1923, Hertha registered 26 patents for her inventions.

One standout invention was the "Ayrton Fan". This was designed to lessen the terrible effects of poisonous gas during World War I (1914–1918). A new, deadly weapon, mustard gas, was causing soldiers' lungs to burn away. Hertha invented a fan to push the gas away from the men. At first, the War Office dismissed her invention, but in the end they issued 104,000 Ayrton Fans to soldiers.

Hertha applied the observations she had made about ripples in water to the movement of air, and invented the Ayrton Fan.

ROYAL SOCIETY

The Royal Society, set up in 1660, is the UK's most important scientific association. In the 1800s, it was definitely an all-male club. By 1902, Hertha's success was too great for the Society to ignore. She was allowed to give a paper, and was nominated to become a Fellow, although the suggestion was turned down. In 1906, the Society awarded her the Hughes Medal for her original work on the movement of ripples in sand and water, and on the electric arc. She is still one of only two women to have received this award.

Lise Meitner

Austrian physicist Lise Meitner is known as the mother of nuclear power. She made her discoveries in the face of prejudice and persecution.

Her discoveries were world-shaking, but Lise is still not as well known as she deserves to be. Elise Meitner was born on 7 November 1878, in the city of Vienna, Austria. From a young age she loved science. She knew that as a girl she would have to fight to keep up her education, but Lise was lucky because her wealthy Jewish parents could support her financially, and she was very determined. She studied physics at the University of Vienna, becoming only the second woman to achieve a PhD in physics there.

NAME: Elise Meitner

BIRTH: 1878, Vienna, Austria

OCCUPATION: Physicist

EDUCATION: University of Vienna

13

66 **Life need not be easy, provided only it was not empty.** **99**

HARD WORK AND HURDLES

In 1907, Lise moved to the University of Berlin in Germany. There she met radiochemist Otto Hahn, and this was the start of a fruitful thirty-year working partnership. As a woman scientist, however, she had a lot of hurdles to overcome. Women could not have paid university jobs, and Lise had to work as an unpaid researcher. Women were not allowed into the labs because they might set their hair on fire! Lise was mocked in the newspapers, which called her a "cosmetic physicist" instead of a "cosmic physicist". Despite all this, Lise won international respect for her work with Hahn.

ATOMIC EXPERIMENTS

With Hahn and Fritz Strassman, Meitner tried bombarding uranium atoms with neutrons, hoping they would stick together to artificially create a new element.

Lise's work at the University of Berlin gained her international recognition. In 1926 she became the first woman in Germany to become a professor of physics.

PHYSICS IN EXILE

In 1933, Adolf Hitler came to power in Germany. State persecution of Jewish people began. Many Jewish scientists emigrated. In 1938, Lise fled to the Netherlands, and then to Sweden. She left all her possessions behind in Germany and took hardly any money. In Sweden, Lise had few resources and nowhere to do experiments. Hahn stayed in Germany. Lise kept in touch with him by letter, and they continued their work together in this way.

Hahn and Strassman continued to work on bombarding uranium atoms with neutrons. They thought they would end up with a new, heavier atom. But instead, they ended up with something lighter. They were puzzled. Lise helped them to understand what their results meant. They had achieved nuclear fission.

Lise co-discovered one element, protactinium, in 1917. Another, meitnerium, was named for her in 1982.

NUCLEAR FISSION

Lise realized that Hahn and Strassman's puzzling results meant that instead of making a new element, they were in fact causing the nucleus of one atom to split apart and release an enormous amount of energy. This process is called nuclear fission.

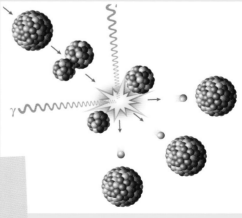

Here a uranium atom's nucleus stretches and splits apart, releasing energy.

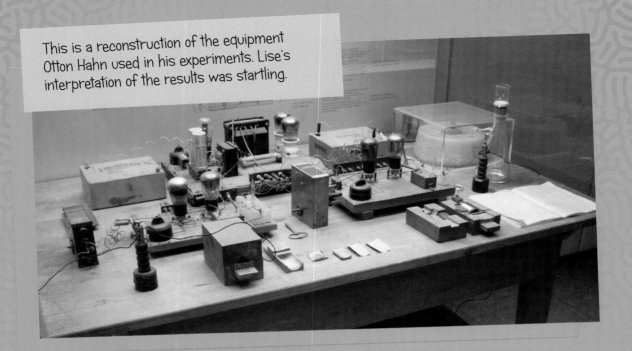

This is a reconstruction of the equipment Otton Hahn used in his experiments. Lise's interpretation of the results was startling.

Lise compared the process of nuclear fission to the stretching of pizza dough.

66 I love physics with all my heart. 99

A WORLD-SHATTERING BREAKTHROUGH

Nuclear fission is a reaction that releases nuclear energy. Its discovery was a huge breakthrough in physics, and with the world on the brink of war its potential was devastatingly important. In 1939, Albert Einstein, who had been following Lise's work, wrote a letter to President Franklin D. Roosevelt, explaining the significance of the discovery and his fears that Germany would make the first atomic bomb.

The US Manhattan Project was set up. It developed the first atomic bomb six years later. Lise turned down an offer from the US to work on the Project, saying "I will have nothing to do with a bomb!"

Lise's understanding of what happens inside atoms led her to be called the "mother of nuclear power".

PEACEFUL POWER

Ironically, Albert Einstein and Lise – two great physicists whose discoveries had enabled the invention of the atomic bomb – were almost the only scientists of their time who did not take part in weapons research. They hated the part they had played in the discovery of such a terrible weapon. Lise spent the rest of her career researching peacetime uses for nuclear power and helped to invent Sweden's first nuclear reactor. She finally retired to England in the 1960s.

NO NOBEL

Lise's research received little recognition at first. Otto Hahn won the 1944 Nobel Prize in Chemistry for work he and Lise had shared. As a Jew in exile, she had not been officially involved in the research, and so was not credited on the published theory. In 1946, she was recognized in the US as Woman of the Year. She later received other awards and honours before her death in England in 1968.

Lise and Otto Hahn worked together in their Berlin lab from 1907 to 1938, and afterwards by correspondence.

maria
Goeppert mayer

Maria Goeppert Mayer was a physicist who was famous for solving the mystery of what happens deep in the heart of atoms.

Maria Goeppert was born in Germany on 28 June 1906. Her father, a scientist, was the sixth generation of university professors in their family – one day, Maria would become the seventh. Young Maria went to a school in Göttingen, Germany, run by suffragettes. Aged 17, she took the university entrance examination along with a few other girls from her school and 30 boys. Only one of the boys passed the exam, but all the girls did!

NAME: Maria Goeppert Mayer

BIRTH: 1906, Kattowitz, Germany (now Katowice, Poland)

OCCUPATION: Physicist

EDUCATION: University of Göttingen

UNIVERSITY SUPERSTAR

Maria began studying maths at the University of Göttingen. She had several women classmates, and there was even a woman professor, Emmy Noether. Maria soon became interested in physics instead of maths, and chose that subject for her PhD. Her PhD thesis was described as a "masterpiece", and she became a superstar at the university.

IN HER HUSBAND'S SHADOW

In 1930, Maria married Joseph Mayer, a fellow physicist. The couple moved to Mayer's home country of the United States, and Joseph became a chemistry professor at John Hopkins University in Maryland. Maria wanted to do the same, but university rules said that professors' wives could not be professors themselves. She was allowed to do some basic office work.

Maria also set up her own lab in an attic for her science work. She worked without pay for nine years, publishing important papers on physics, quantum mechanics and chemistry.

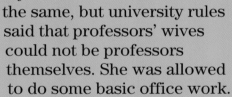

Bright young physicists Joseph and Maria set off for a new life in the United States in 1930.

Maria in 1963 – the year she won the Nobel Prize.

GOVERNMENT SCIENTIST

In 1941, Maria was offered her first paid teaching post at a private college. The US government noticed her scientific skills and experience, and in 1943 she was asked to join the Manhattan Project, the research effort that led to the development of the atomic bomb. She led a small team changing raw uranium into weapons-quality uranium.

After World War II (1939–1945) Joseph and Maria moved to Chicago, and Maria was appointed professor at the University of Chicago. Suddenly, she was a nuclear scientist! This was a new and exciting area of physics, and Maria worked on trying to solve some of its greatest challenges.

When asked why girls needed to study science, Maria would reply with another question: "Do girls only have to learn how to read just to study cookbooks?"

66 Winning the prize wasn't half as exciting as doing the work itself. 99

THE NUCLEAR SHELL MODEL

After painstaking research, Maria came up with a model for the structure of atoms, called the nuclear shell model. Her model explains that protons and neutrons are arranged in rings or shells inside the nucleus, like layers of an onion.

Maria realized that the protons and neutrons move around independently in the different layers, with different levels of energy. She described this as being like pairs of dancers waltzing in a ballroom, some of them spinning clockwise and some of them spinning anticlockwise. She worked out that certain numbers of protons and neutrons make a more stable arrangement than others. These numbers are called "magic numbers".

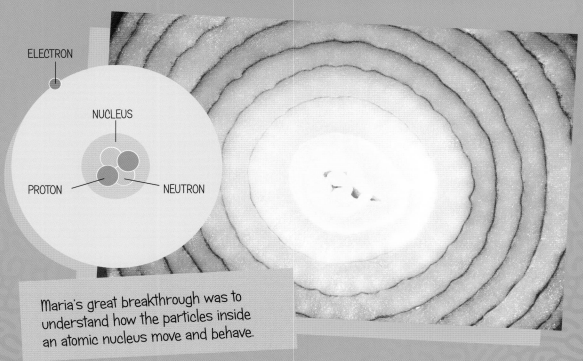

ELECTRON

NUCLEUS

PROTON   NEUTRON

Maria's great breakthrough was to understand how the particles inside an atomic nucleus move and behave.

This 2011 US postage stamp honours Maria's work. There is also a crater on Venus named after her.

NOBEL PRIZE

Three other German scientists, Otto Haxel, J. Hans D. Jensen and Hans Suess, were investigating the same problem at the same time as Maria. All reached the same conclusion, and they announced their findings just before Maria did. In 1963 Maria, Jensen and Eugene Wigner shared the Nobel Prize in Physics for their amazing discoveries regarding nuclear shell structure. She died after suffering a heart attack in 1972.

Only three women have won the Nobel Prize in Physics: Marie Curie. Maria and Donna Strickland.

ISOTOPES

A lot of Maria's work was on isotopes. To understand them, we need to know that atoms contain a nucleus, which is itself made up of particles called protons and neutrons. Isotopes are different forms of the same element, having the same number of protons but a different number of neutrons. Different isotopes often behave differently, and some are more useful than others. Maria worked on finding out why this is.

Lillian Gilbreth

> Lillian Gilbreth was the first woman to work as an industrial engineer. Her unusual approach to science led to improvements in all our daily lives.

Lillian's insights revolutionized workplaces and homes. Born in Oakland, California, USA, on 24 May 1878, Lillian Moller was a bright girl who graduated high school with good grades. To continue studying, she had to persuade her father that she could cope with the work while also helping out at home. She studied English literature at the University of California and later studied for and gained a PhD in psychology from Brown University. This was an unusual route into engineering, but it allowed her to see things differently and fed her ability for clever innovations.

24

Lillian was one of the first "superwomen" who combined a successful career with raising her children.

PROBLEM-SOLVING PARTNERS

Lillian married Frank Gilbreth, an industrial engineer. Frank was interested in discovering ways to make bricklaying faster and easier, and Lillian got interested in the problem too. Together they would study a task and break it down into pieces. They observed things like workers' posture and how workers tired during a day. They came up with ideas to make the workers' jobs quicker and easier.

PIONEER INDUSTRIAL PSYCHOLOGIST

There was no such thing as an industrial psychologist before Lillian. Industrial psychologists study workers' behaviour and attitude, and their relationships with each other, as a way to work out improvements. The Gilbreths ran a business advising companies how to manage people and tasks so that employees would be happier and more work would get done.

Lillian and Frank wrote many books about their findings, but often publishers insisted that only Frank's name went on the cover.

CHEAPER BY THE DOZEN

Lillian and Frank had 12 children, and the kids often took part in the Gilbreths' experiments, finding faster and more efficient ways to wash dishes, or to brush teeth, for example. The book *Cheaper by the Dozen* tells the story of this unconventional home life. It was turned into a film in 1950.

Lillian and Frank with 11 of their children in the 1920s.

ENGINEERING THE HOME

Lillian and Frank didn't just investigate building sites and factories – they studied the home as well. In the 1920s, housework such as cooking and cleaning could keep women busy all day. Lillian studied all these tasks in detail, coming up with ideas and inventions that would make these jobs quicker and easier, freeing women to do other things, such as paid work outside the home.

Frank died in 1924, and Lillian took charge of their business. At first, many customers didn't want a woman telling them how to run their factories, but slowly Lillian convinced companies to use her. For New York department store Macy's, she spent time working as a sales clerk in order to help Macy's understand what it was like for the shop workers. Her observations and suggestions meant the rate of work improved.

Lillian herself hated kitchen tasks, especially cooking. No wonder she put her energy into making them less trouble for everyone!

27

> ❝ Under [Mother's] arrangement, a person could mix a cake, put it in the oven and do the dishes, without taking more than a couple of dozen steps. ❞
>
> The Gilbreth children

THE "WORK TRIANGLE"

Concentrating on the home, again Lillian broke everything down into pieces. One piece was the layout of the kitchen. She came up with the idea of the "work triangle" between the fridge, sink and hob. People doing kitchen jobs need to move between these three things all the time. Lillian designed a kitchen with these things close together, to cut down on lots of wasted energy walking about. She tested her new design by making a strawberry shortcake, and took less than one-sixth of the number of steps it would have taken in an old kitchen!

Lillian kept on working at inventions for the home. She interviewed over 4,000 women to figure out the best height for sinks, hobs and other kitchen equipment.

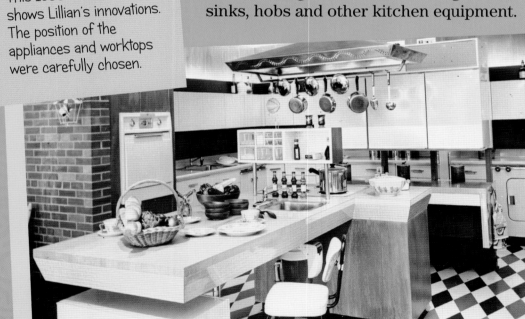

This 1956 "modern" kitchen shows Lillian's innovations. The position of the appliances and worktops were carefully chosen.

The arrangement of shelves inside a fridge. especially the egg keeper and butter tray. owes a lot to Lillian's work.

She also invented the foot-pedal rubbish bin and the shelves inside refrigerator doors, and created an improved can opener.

SPREADING HER IDEAS

Lillian taught her methods, called scientific management, and they became a respected way of managing and improving the workplace or home. She gained recognition for her incredible achievements. In 1950, she was the first honourary member of the Society of Women Engineers. In 1964, at the age of 86, she got a job at the respected Massachusetts Institute of Technology. In 1965, she was the first woman elected to the National Academy of Engineering, and the next year won the Hoover Medal, an engineering prize. She died in 1972.

Lillian designed adaptations to help disabled people at home or enable them to go to work. This helped win her the Hoover Medal.

Hedy Lamarr

Hedy Lamarr was a Hollywood film star and a star inventor too. Her invention paved the way for the communications systems we all rely on today.

Hedwig Kiesler was born on 9 November 1914, in Vienna, Austria. By the age of 17, she was an actor appearing in her first movie. Her dream was to leave her home country and her first husband, and move to Hollywood, United States. In 1938, this dream became a reality. She signed a contract with MGM Studios and changed her name to Hedy Lamarr. Her Hollywood life had begun.

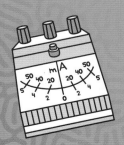

> **" Any girl can be glamorous. All you have to do is stand still and look stupid. "**

HOLLYWOOD STAR
Hedy's career took off and she became a film star. She appeared with some of the most popular actors of the 1940s. She was admired as one of the most beautiful and talented leading ladies in Hollywood – but she was unimpressed by the praise she received for her beauty.

HIDDEN TALENT
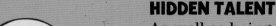

As well as being a successful actor, Hedy had a surprising hobby as an inventor. She had her own workshop, where she experimented with ideas and inventions.

Back in Austria, Hedy's first husband had been a weapons manufacturer. She had overheard secrets about military equipment when people thought she was not listening or that she would not understand what they were talking about.

Hedy as a film star. Some people say she found her acting roles boring, and turned to inventing for a challenge.

A US Navy ship firing torpedoes during World War II.

During World War II (1939–1945), Hedy thought she could solve a military problem and help with the war effort.

ACTRESS + COMPOSER = INVENTORS

The US Navy's most advanced torpedoes were guided by radio signals. Radio signals could be jammed easily by the enemy, which could make the torpedoes go off course. Hedy put her mind to the challenge. She teamed up with a Hollywood friend, the music composer George Antheil, and together they worked to solve the problem. They realized that a radio signal could change frequencies like a piano player changes musical notes, which would make it impossible to jam the signal.

Hedy also invented an improved traffic light, and a tablet that would make water fizzy.

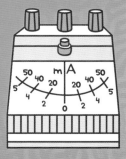

33

When she was honoured with the Electronic Frontier Foundation Pioneer Award, Hedy is said to have joked, "It's about time."

FHSS TECHNOLOGY

Hedy and George invented a secret communication system called the frequency-hopping spread spectrum (FHSS). In this system, radio communications switch frequencies, following a pre-planned pattern. The sender and receiver know the pattern, but no one from outside can listen in or jam the signal. Hedy and George received a patent for the invention in 1942 – the patent was donated to the US military, but Navy bosses did not grasp how useful it could be and put the idea aside.

NAVY USE

In 1962, at the time of the Cuban Missile Crisis, an updated version of Hedy and Antheil's FHSS system was used on US Navy ships.

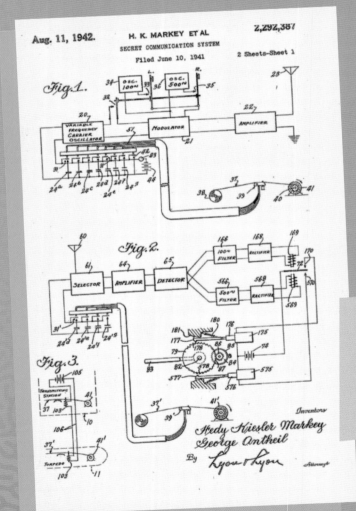

This patent, filed by Hedy Lamarr and George Anteil in 1941, detailed their "secret communication system".

THE "OSCARS" OF INVENTING

Hedy and Antheil's invention paved the way for developing the technology used in the communication systems we now take for granted every day.

Decades after their work, the widespread use of Bluetooth and Wi-Fi technology meant people finally understood the importance of what Lamarr and Antheil had achieved. They began to get recognition. Antheil died in 1959, but in 1997 they received the Electronic Frontier Foundation Pioneer Award and the Bulbie Gnass Spirit of Achievement Award (known as the "Oscars" of inventing). Hedy was the award's first female winner. Hedy died in 2000. In 2014, although after their deaths, Hedy and Antheil were inducted into the National Inventors Hall of Fame.

Antheil had composed for automatic, self-playing pianos. The FHSS used motor-driven rolls like those in self-playing pianos.

SMART TECHNOLOGY

Hedy and Antheil's invention made the modern boom in digital communications possible. Versions of their invention are used in Wi-Fi, barcode scanners, digital mobile phone technology, email and Bluetooth technology.

When you surf the Web, Hedy is one of the people you have to thank!

The "Ladies' Bridge"
and
Rosie the Riveter

A bridge rebuilt largely by women labourers and a poster-girl machine operator were part of a wave of women taking on heavy "men's work" during wartime.

During World War II (1939–1945), women everywhere stepped up to fill the jobs left by men who had gone to fight. In London, UK, one of the city's main bridges was built almost entirely by women, but the secret of the "Ladies' Bridge" is only now starting to unfold. On the other side of the Atlantic, in the United States, millions of women were inspired by a fictional character, a stylish, capable, strong machine operator named Rosie the Riveter, who shouted "We Can Do It!"

QUICK FACTS
....
NAME: Waterloo Bridge, nicknamed the "Ladies' Bridge"

BUILT: 1817, London, UK, rebuilt 1942–1945

QUICK FACTS
....
NAME: Rosie the Riveter

CREATED: 1942, Pittsburgh, Pennsylvania, USA

OCCUPATION: Fictional machine worker and cultural icon

> **66 He said, 'No, you never done any welding!' ... He didn't believe it, couldn't believe it, but it was perfectly true. 99**

Edith, born 1907, London

When World War II broke out, Waterloo Bridge in London was in a bad state of repair, and rebuilding was already underway. But in 1941, thousands of men were sent away to fight. This resulted in a labour crisis.

FEMALE WORKFORCE

Women had to fill all sorts of jobs left vacant by men who had gone to war. Jobs included making ammunition, weapons and aircraft. Films and posters praised women's work on farms, on transport and in factories. But the many thousands who started work as construction workers went mainly unnoticed.

SECRET WORK

All through the war years, women worked alongside men to rebuild Waterloo Bridge. They worked as general labourers, concrete workers, stonemasons, welders, carpenters and joiners and bricklayers. Until very recently, few people knew about this.

Waterloo Bridge in London today.

This picture of women welders is one of very few so far discovered that show the workers on the "Ladies' Bridge".

At the time, perhaps people just didn't notice they were women! Women's work clothes were just like men's work clothes. All information about the bridge was kept top secret because it was important to the war. The new bridge was opened in 1945, with a speech that thanked "the fortunate men who built this bridge". No mention was made of the women.

TELLING THE STORY

A lot is known about the women who worked in factories, on farms, on buses and railroads, and even those who worked as engineers, code-breakers and spies. But little is known about the women who worked on the "Ladies' Bridge". Historians are searching for more evidence. So far there are just two or three photos, and no written history. Hopefully some of the women involved in this project, or the men who worked with them, are still alive – and the full story can be told.

For decades, boatmen running tourist boats on London's River Thames were the only people who used the name "The Ladies' Bridge" and talked about the female labourers who built it.

> **❝ I was a Rosie the Riveter. I'm really proud of that. ❞**
>
> Ruth Duccini,
> *Wizard of Oz* actor

INSPIRING ICON

Rosie the Riveter wasn't even a real person, but she inspired millions of Americans. She was created to encourage women to take up heavy "men's work" during World War II. Housewives were told that if they could use an electric mixer, they could use a drill. Millions answered the call, with six million women producing ammunition and building ships and aeroplanes during the war years. There were several versions of this strong, capable-looking character. The name Rosie the Riveter was first used in 1942. There were songs and even a film about her.

SOCIAL CHANGE?

Women proved to themselves and to the nation that they could do "men's work", and they could do it well, and still care for their families.

We Can Do It!

POST FEB. 15 TO FEB. 28

WAR PRODUCTION CO-ORDINATING COMMITTEE

The most famous version of Rosie is the 1942 "Westinghouse Poster". with the empowering slogan. "We Can Do It!"

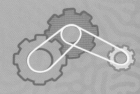

Workers got together to share jobs such as housework and childcare. After the war, things changed. Government posters urged women to return to the home and to their lower-paid "women's" jobs. Many were happy to get back to normal, but some wanted to keep their new jobs, newfound freedom and better pay. The millions of "Rosies" had shown what women could do.

"Rosies" did all sorts of heavy engineering jobs. One was riveting – fitting rivets (flat pins that fasten pieces of metal together).

FEMINIST ICON

Rosie is an icon of feminism even today. People still use her image to show that women are strong and that they still need to fight for women's rights. In January 2017, there were huge Women's March events all round the world – there were probably hundreds of marchers dressed as Rosie! For this magazine cover illustrating the march, the artist chose to make Rosie African American, to highlight how people were standing up for minority rights as well as for women's rights.

The New Yorker magazine's February 2017 cover shows how powerful the image of Rosie can still be.

Timeline

1715	Sybilla Masters is the first woman in the USA to get a patent for an invention, which cleans and processes corn.
1826	America's first public high schools for girls open in Boston and New York.
1870	Emily Roebling steps up to become chief engineer on the construction of Brooklyn Bridge in New York City.
1888	Bertha Benz with her husband Karl makes the first long-distance road trip, and invents brake pads along the way.
1890s	Hertha Ayrton invents a new electric arc light, and becomes the first female member of the UK's Institution of Electrical Engineers.
1903	Mary Andersen invents the windshield wiper.
1906	Hertha Ayrton wins the Hughes Medal.
1914–1918	World War I. Hertha Ayrton's Ayrton Fan is one of the inventions that aims to reduce soldiers' suffering.
1918	Women over the age of 30 in the UK win the right to vote. (Other women only get voting rights in 1921.) Women in Germany also gain the right to vote, but women in the USA have to wait until 1920.
1920s	Lillian Gilbreth revolutionizes kitchen design.
1939	Katharine Burr Blodgett's invisible, non-reflecting glass is used to film smash-hit film *Gone With the Wind*.
1939–1945	World War II. Women step up to fill jobs traditionally done by men, including heavy engineering work.

1940s	Lise Meitner discovers nuclear fission.
1942	Hedy Lamarr and George Antheil develop their secret communications system or FHSS.
1947	Edith Clarke becomes the United States' first female professor of electrical engineering.
1948	Mária Telkes' team builds the first 100 per cent solar heating system.
1960s	Ursula Franklin studies the effects of nuclear blast fallout.
1963	Maria Goeppert Mayer, Hans D. Jensen and Eugene Wigner win the Nobel Prize in Physics for their work on the structure of atoms, known as the nuclear shell model.
1966	Chien-Shiung Wu publishes her nuclear physics textbook *Beta Decay*.
1973	Nuclear physicist Shirley Jackson becomes the first African American woman to earn a PhD – in any subject – from Massachusetts Institute of Technology (MIT).
1990s	Cynthia Breazeal engineers Kismet, the first "social robot" that can imitate human emotion.
1999	Wi-Fi technology is launched.
2001	Lene Hau stops a beam of light completely.
2016	Fabiola Gianotti becomes the first female director of CERN, the world-leading particle physics laboratory in Geneva, Switzerland.

Gallery

The scientists covered in this book are only a few of the women who have advanced the study of physics and engineering, but here are more who achieved great things.

Emily Roebling (1803—1903)

The first female field engineer, Emily stepped up to this role in 1870 when her husband Washington Roebling, chief engineer on the construction of Brooklyn Bridge in New York City, was paralyzed. Emily, who had learned about bridge construction alongside her husband, took over the day-to-day supervision of the project.

Bertha Benz (1849-1944)

Bertha Benz and her husband Karl owned the car company Benz. One day in 1888, Bertha took off on the first long-distance road trip, travelling 106 km (66 miles) in 12 hours. Along the way she made several repairs and fixes, and when the car's brakes started to fail she went to a shoemaker and had him make some leather brake pads – so co-inventing brake pads too.

Mária Telkes (1900-1995)

Nicknamed the "sun queen" for her work in solar energy research, Hungarian-American Mária Telkes led a project to build the first 100 per cent solar heating system for a house. She also invented a solar still – a piece of equipment used on life rafts to convert seawater into safe drinking water.

Chien-Shiung Wu (1912-1997)

Chien-Shiung Wu grew up in China at a time when most girls did not get an education. But she became a professor of experimental physics in the US. She worked on the Manhattan Project, worked out how radioactive atoms decay and discovered a new particle.

Shirley Jackson (born 1946)

The first African American woman to earn a PhD from MIT, Shirley Jackson was Chairman of the US Nuclear Regulatory Commission. She moved into telecommunications and made breakthroughs that paved the way for the portable fax, touch tone telephone, solar cells, fibre optic cables, and more.

Donna Strickland (born 1959)

Canadian physicist Donna Strickland won the 2018 Nobel Prize in Physics for her work with lasers. She invented a way of making very short, high-powered laser pulses. The method is already being used in industry and for eye surgery.

Cynthia Breazeal (born 1967)

A pioneer of robot technology, engineer Cynthia Breazeal works on making robots that can learn from people. Her invention Nexi, a human-like robot, was named one of *Time* magazine's best inventions of 2008. She won the Gilbreth Lecture Award – named after Lillian Gilbreth – in 2008.

SCIENCE NOW

In physics today, thousands of scientists are researching the particles that make up the universe, for example by trying to recreate the conditions immediately following the "Big Bang" so we can learn more about how the universe works. In engineering, innovations range from self-driving cars and new rocket launch systems to 3-D printing and new, cheap solar cells. Today, there are more than 900,000 women working in STEM in the UK. Things have improved a lot in the last 50 years, and it's exciting to see what comes next.

What interests you most about physics and engineering? Would you like to find out about the mysteries of matter or use existing technologies to improve the gadgets we use every day? To find out how to get into science, visit STEM information sites, such as the WISE campaign at **www.wisecampaign.org.uk**

Glossary

ammunition bullets, grenades, shells and bombs

arc a glowing flow of electricity across a gap

architect a person who designs buildings

atom a tiny particle that is the basic unit of matter

atomic bomb a bomb in which the explosive power is caused by the release of energy from splitting atoms, also called a nuclear bomb

Cuban Missile Crisis the 13-day period in 1962 when the Soviet Union installed nuclear missiles in Cuba, and the US blockaded the island

evaporation when a liquid turns into a gas

Fellow a member of an organization such as a scientific society

feminism the belief that women and girls should have the same rights and opportunities as men and boys, and the effort to make this happen

frequency a measurement of the number of times a sound wave vibrates in a period of time

governess a woman employed to live with a family and teach the children

isotopes atoms that have the same number of protons but different numbers of neutrons

neutron a type of particle found in an atom's nucleus

Nobel Prize a very prestigious prize, awarded for work in science, literature, economics and peace

nuclear fission the process of splitting an atom's nucleus, which releases a huge amount of energy

nucleus the centre part of an atom, consisting of protons and neutrons

oxidation reacting with oxygen

patent a document that gives a person or company the right to be the only producer of something, such as an invention or a drug, for a time

persecution cruel or unfair treatment of people

psychologist someone who studies the human mind and behaviour

quantum mechanics a branch of physics

Wi-Fi a type of communications technology that uses radio signals

Further resources

Books

Can You Feel The Force? Big Questions About Physics, Richard Hammond (Dorling Kindersley, 2006)

Physics: Why Matter Matters! (Basher Science), Simon Basher and Dan Green (Kingfisher, 2008)

Trailblazers: 33 Women in Science Who Changed the World, Rachel Swaby (Random House Book for Young Readers, 2016)

Women in Science: 50 Fearless Pioneers Who Changed the World, Rachel Ignotofsky (Wren & Rook, 2017)

Websites

www.ducksters.com/science/physics/
A site for kids with helpful articles on key physics topics.

gizmodo.com/these-17-women-changed-the-face-of-physics-1689043918
A great list of women physicists (including some astronomers, mathematicians and others).

www.theladiesbridge.co.uk
Lots of information about the "Ladies' Bridge", including interviews with World War II labourers and a documentary film.

www.tomorrowsengineers.org.uk
A wealth of information and resources about what you need for a career in engineering.

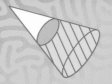

index